T0010745

Searchlight BOOKS™

World Traveler

Travel to India

Matt Doeden

Lerner Publications ◆ Minneapolis

Content consultant: Meraj Ahmed, PhD, director, Hindi-Urdu languages, Asian and Middle Eastern studies, University of Minnesota

Lerner Publications Company
An imprint of Lerner Publishing Group, Inc.
241 First Avenue North
Minneapolis, MN 55401 USA

For reading levels and more information, look up this title
at www.lernerbooks.com.

Main body text set in Adrianna Regular.
Typeface provided by Chank.

Photo Editor: Cynthia Zemlicka
Lerner team: Sue Marquis

Library of Congress Cataloging-in-Publication Data

Names: Doeden, Matt, author.
Title: Travel to India / Matt Doeden.
Description: Minneapolis: Lerner Publications, [2022] | Series: Searchlight books - world traveler | Includes bibliographical references and index. | Audience: Ages 8–11 | Audience: Grades 4–6 | Summary: "Readers are in for a treat when they visit India through this book's pages! They'll discover what it's like to live in modern India, plus learn about the country's history, geography, culture, and more"—Provided by publisher.
Identifiers: LCCN 2021022730 (print) | LCCN 2021022731 (ebook) | ISBN 9781728441696 (lib. bdg.) | ISBN 9781728448817 (pbk.) | ISBN 9781728444994 (eb pdf)
Subjects: LCSH: India—Juvenile literature.
Classification: LCC DS407 .D64 2022 (print) | LCC DS407 (ebook) | DDC 954—dc23

LC record available at https://lccn.loc.gov/2021022730
LC ebook record available at https://lccn.loc.gov/2021022731

Manufactured in the United States of America
1-49924-49767-9/1/2021

Table of Contents

Chapter 1

GEOGRAPHY AND CLIMATE . . . 4

Chapter 2

HISTORY AND GOVERNMENT . . . 10

Chapter 3

CULTURE AND PEOPLE . . . 17

Chapter 4

DAILY LIFE . . . 23

Map and Key Facts • 29
Glossary • 30
Learn More • 31
Index • 32

Chapter 1

GEOGRAPHY AND CLIMATE

The Indian landscape is beautiful and varied. India boasts lowland coasts, fertile plains, and the towering Himalayas.

The Land

India, the world's seventh-largest country, covers 1,269,219 square miles (3,287,262 sq. km). India borders China, Nepal, Bhutan, Bangladesh, and Myanmar on the northeast. Its northwestern neighbor is Pakistan. The Arabian Sea lies to India's west. To the east is the Bay of Bengal. Both bodies of water are part of the Indian Ocean.

India is part of Asia. The Himalayas, the highest mountain range in the world, forms the border between India and its neighbors to the northeast. South of the Himalayas is the low-lying Indo-Gangetic Plain. The land there is flat and fertile. Farther south, a peninsula juts into the Indian Ocean. This peninsula includes the Deccan plateau, a stretch of high, flat land.

The Himalayas dominate the skyline in northern India.

Mountains

The Himalayas stretch across northern India. The tallest mountains in the world are in this range. India's highest peak is Kanchenjunga. It rises 28,169 feet (8,586 m) above sea level. Kanchenjunga is the world's third-highest mountain.

The Satpura, Vindhya, Aravalli, and Western and Eastern Ghats mountain ranges are also in India.

Kanchenjunga is the tallest mountain in India.

Must-See Stop:
Great Himalayan National Park

The Great Himalayan National Park is a fantastic place to see India's mountain wildlife. The rugged mountain landscape is home to brown bears, musk deer, snow leopards, and many more animals. Vehicles aren't allowed in the park, but visitors can hike trails there. They will be rewarded with spectacular views of glaciers, mountain valleys, and green meadows.

Flamingos at Chilika Lake

Rivers and Lakes

Major rivers in India include the Brahmaputra and the Ganges. The Indus River gives India its name. This river begins in China, crosses Indian-held territory, and then flows through Pakistan.

Vembanad is the longest lake in India. This narrow lake stretches 60 miles (97 km) along India's southwestern coast. Chilika Lake is a coastal lake in eastern India. More than fifty streams feed this body of water. The lake is home to many birds.

Climate

Weather in India varies from place to place. Winter, or Shishir, is usually the coolest time of year. It lasts from January to mid-February. Spring, or Vasant Ritu, runs from mid-February into April. Then comes summer, or Grishma Ritu. This season can be very hot and humid. It lasts to June.

Varsha Ritu, from June to mid-August, brings heavy monsoons to much of India. These rains taper off and the weather cools in autumn, or Sharad Ritu. This season lasts from mid-August through September. Hemant Ritu, or prewinter, runs from October through December.

Chapter 2

HISTORY AND GOVERNMENT

People have called India home for thousands of years. A civilization developed in the Indus River valley, in northwestern India, around 2300 BCE. The people there built cities and created systems for writing and counting.

Around 1500 BCE, people came to India from central Asia. This group, called the Aryans, settled into villages and tended livestock. They eventually spread their culture across most of India.

A Changing India

Many of the world's biggest religions started in India. Hinduism started in the Indus River valley sometime between 2300 and 1500 BCE. Buddhism, Jainism, and Sikhism also began in India.

India's Golden Age (300 to 600 CE) was a time of peace and prosperity. Art, science, and religion all thrived then.

An Indian ruler built this temple complex in the fifteenth century.

Over the centuries, many settlers and invaders came to India. They brought new ideas and religious faiths. These included Christianity and Islam. At times, people of different faiths lived and worked in peace. But sometimes they fought.

Foreign Powers

In the 1500s, European merchants came to India. They bought silk, spices, and other valuables. Spain, Portugal, and Britain started colonies there. In 1599, English

AN ISLAMIC HOUSE OF WORSHIP IN THE CITY OF DELHI

This painting from the 1760s shows a meeting between British and Indian soldiers.

merchants formed the British East India Company. It imported Indian goods to Europe. It also gained political power in parts of India. In 1858, the British took full control of India.

New Leaders

India's people were unhappy under British control. They wanted to rule their own nation. Leaders in the fight for independence included Mohammed Ali Jinnah and Mohandas Gandhi.

Gandhi became famous for leading nonviolent protests. To oppose British control, he encouraged Indians to march peacefully and to boycott British goods.

After World War II (1939–1945), India achieved independence. Leaders also split the nation into two parts—India and Pakistan. Most of the people in India were Hindus. The Pakistani people were mostly Muslims.

Mohandas Gandhi (*center*) led nonviolent protests against British rule.

Indian lawmakers meet in 2021.

Government

India is divided into twenty-eight states and eight territories. People elect local leaders. They also vote for leaders to represent them in India's federal government.

The federal government has three branches. The legislative branch makes laws. It has two lawmaking bodies, the Rajya Sabha (Council of States) and the Lok Sabha (House of the People). India's president and prime minister lead the executive branch of government. This branch carries out the nation's laws. The judicial branch consists of courts and judges. They make sure that laws are enforced fairly. The Supreme Court is India's highest court.

Let's Celebrate:
Independence Day

Every year on August 15, India celebrates its independence from Britain. All around the country, people raise Indian flags and march in or watch parades. Political leaders give speeches. People also decorate homes and other buildings in colorful lights.

Indians celebrate Independence Day.

Chapter 3

CULTURE AND PEOPLE

About 72 percent of Indians are of Aryan descent. Their ancestors were among India's earliest people. The Dravidians were also early inhabitants of India. Scientists don't know much about their origins. Dravidians make up about 25 percent of the population. Most of them live in southern India. Other groups make up the remaining 3 percent.

▲

THIS WALL PAINTING SHOWS VISHNU, A HINDU GOD.

Religion

Over the years, India has been a place of religious diversity. About 80 percent of modern Indians are Hindu. Hindus believe in many gods. The beliefs and practices are written in sacred books.

Many Muslims moved from India to Pakistan after the nations split in 1947. But India is still home to many Muslims. About 14 percent of modern Indians follow Islam. Christians and Sikhs each make up about

2 percent of India's population. Much smaller numbers practice other religions.

Language and Writing

More than twenty different languages are spoken in India. Two of the most common are Hindi and Urdu. Many people speak Hindi-Urdu, a blended language.

English is common in India. It is widely used in business, government, and education.

This street sign in Delhi is written in Hindi.

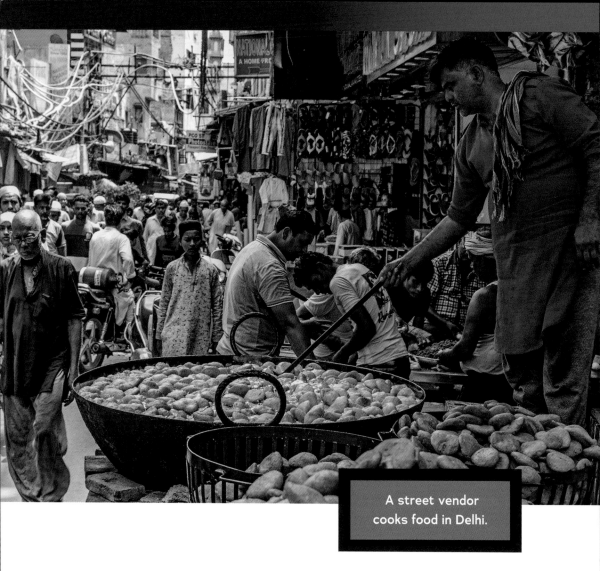

A street vendor cooks food in Delhi.

Food and Art

Indian people enjoy lots of different foods. Cooks use vegetables such as peas, cabbage, and carrots. Meals also include rice and other grains. Lamb and chicken are common meats. Many dishes are flavored with local spices, such as mustard, cardamom, and turmeric. South India is famous for its spicy curry dishes.

India has a rich artistic heritage. Many paintings and statues show Hindu gods. Madhubani is a painting style that features colorful shapes and patterns. Tanjore-style paintings have gold foil on top of paint. The nation has a popular film industry, often called Bollywood.

A Bollywood film crew

Must-See Stop:
Taj Mahal

The city of Agra is home to one of the most famous tourist attractions in the world—the Taj Mahal. Emperor Shah Jahan had it built as a tomb for his favorite wife, Mumtaz Mahal. Completed about 1650, the beautiful white marble building is surrounded by gardens and pools. This work of art attracts millions of visitors every year.

Chapter 4

DAILY LIFE

Modern India is home to more than 1.3 billion people. China is the only nation with more people. About 35 percent of India's people live in large urban areas. Mumbai, Delhi, and Bangalore are its largest cities.

Education is important to India's people. All Indian children six to fourteen must go to school. About 74 percent of India's people can read. To help their families earn a living, many students leave school to take jobs or work on family farms.

Future Challenges

India has a large and powerful economy. People there work in technology, manufacturing, and farming. Yet much of the nation's wealth lies with just a small group of people. Meanwhile, vast numbers of Indians live below the poverty line.

Indian factory workers assemble electronics.

Let's Celebrate:
Diwali

Indians celebrate many holidays. One of them is Diwali. This five-day annual festival takes place in October or November. Diwali started out as a celebration of Hindu gods and heroes. But

Indians of other faiths have also embraced it. Families decorate their homes with lights for the celebration. They gather with friends and family for parties filled with food, dancing, and more.

Health is another big concern in India. Providing food and clean water for all citizens is challenging. In big cities, many people live close together. In crowded communities, disease can spread fast. That happened in 2020 and 2021, when COVID-19 spread throughout India.

The city of Delhi,
photographed from the air

Indian classmates pose for a photo.

With its growing economy, India is becoming a world superpower. Its people are working hard to solve problems and to create a bright future.

Map and Key Facts

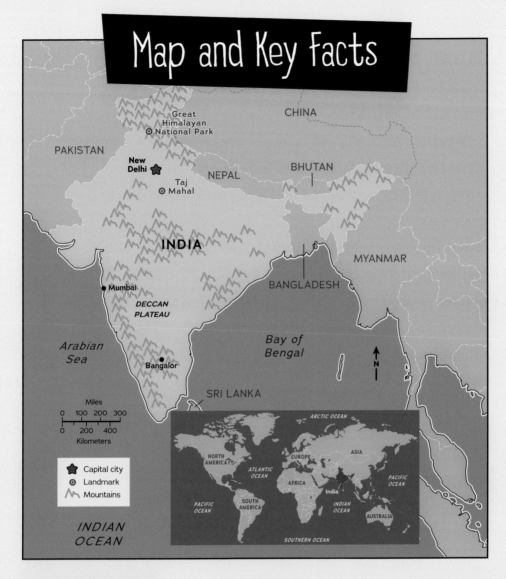

- Great Himalayan National Park
- CHINA
- PAKISTAN
- New Delhi ★
- Taj Mahal
- NEPAL
- BHUTAN
- INDIA
- MYANMAR
- Mumbai
- BANGLADESH
- DECCAN PLATEAU
- Arabian Sea
- Bay of Bengal
- Bangalor
- N
- SRI LANKA

Miles
0 100 200 300

0 200 400
Kilometers

★ Capital city
⊙ Landmark
⋀ Mountains

INDIAN OCEAN

ARCTIC OCEAN
NORTH AMERICA
EUROPE
ASIA
ATLANTIC OCEAN
AFRICA
India
PACIFIC OCEAN
PACIFIC OCEAN
SOUTH AMERICA
INDIAN OCEAN
AUSTRALIA
SOUTHERN OCEAN

Flag of India

- **Continent: Asia**
- **Capital city: New Delhi**
- **Population: 1.3 billion**
- **Languages: Hindi, Urdu, Hindi-Urdu, English, and other languages**

29

Glossary

boycott: to refuse to do business with an individual, organization, or country

civilization: a society with a government, social organization, communications systems, and technology

curry: a dish of vegetables and often meat cooked in a spicy sauce

federal government: the central government of a nation

fertile: good for growing crops

glacier: a large mass of ice that moves slowly over the land

import: to bring from one country to another for sale

monsoon: a seasonal wind that brings very heavy rainfall

nonviolent protest: speaking out for change without harming anyone

peninsula: an area of land that sticks out into a body of water

plateau: an area of high, flat land

Learn More

Britannica Kids: India
    https://kids.britannica.com/kids/article/India/345707

Faust, Daniel R. *Ancient India.* New York: Gareth Stevens, 2019.

Fehlen, Douglas J. *Explore Delhi.* Mankato, MN: 12-Story Library, 2020.

National Geographic Kids: India
    https://kids.nationalgeographic.com/geography/countries/article/india

Quinlan, Julia J. *Hinduism.* New York: Rosen, 2019.

Taj Mahal
    https://www.tajmahal.gov.in

Index

Aryans, 10, 17

Bollywood, 21

Britain, 12–14, 16

Diwali, 25

Dravidians, 17

Gandhi, Mohandas, 14

Himalayas, 4–6

Hindi, 19

Hinduism, 11, 14, 18, 21, 25

independence, 14, 16

Islam, 12, 18

monsoon, 9

Pakistan, 4, 8, 14, 18

Taj Mahal, 22

Urdu, 19

Photo Acknowledgments

Image credits: Asada Nami/Shutterstock.com, p. 5; Emad Aljumah/Getty Images, p. 6; Denis Vostrikov/Getty Images, p. 7; Keren Su/Getty Images, p. 8; prudhvichowdary/Shutterstock.com, p. 11; travelview/Shutterstock.com, p. 12; PRISMA ARCHIVO/Alamy Stock Photo, p. 13; Universal History Archive/Getty Images, p. 14; Raj K Raj/Hindustan Times/Getty Images, p. 15; Rakesh Roul/Shutterstock.com, p. 16; Boris Stroujko/Shutterstock.com, p. 18; PhotographerIncognito/Shutterstock.com, p. 19; Mahesh M J/Shutterstock.com, p. 20; Olga Vasilyeva/Shutterstock.com, p. 21; RuthChoi/Shutterstock.com, p. 22; PradeepGaurs/Shutterstock.com, p. 24; IndiaPix/IndiaPicture/Getty Images, p. 25; Sanga Park/Getty Images, pp. 26–27; CRS PHOTO/Shutterstock.com, p. 28; Laura Westlund, p. 29.

Cover: Smarta/Shutterstock.com.